Walt Disney

HIS LIFE IN PICTURES

Edited by Russell Schroeder

Photographs from The Walt Disney Archives
Quoted Material Drawn from Interviews with Walt Disney

Introduction by Diane Disney Miller

Disney
PRESS

New York

Art direction by Kenneth Shue.

Designed by Janice Kawamoto.

The drawings found on pages 10 through 15 are original cartoons
created by Walt Disney. The remaining pieces of artwork in the
book are actual animation drawings used in the creation of the
Walt Disney Studio's animated films.

Oscar® and Academy Award® are registered trademarks of
the Motion Picture Academy and are used by permission.

Disneyland®, Walt Disney World®, and EPCOT® are registered
trademarks of The Walt Disney Company.

Copyright © 1996 by Disney Press.

Printed in the United States of America.

First Edition
10 9 8 7 6 5 4 3 2 1

This book is set in Times Roman and Futura.
Library of Congress Catalog Card Number has been applied for.
ISBN: 0-7868-3116-2 (trade)
ISBN: 0-7868-5043-4 (lib. bdg.)

C ONTENTs

INTRODUCTION

My sister Sharon and I sensed that our father was special long before we realized that he was famous.

He drove us to school every morning—from kindergarten until we were licensed drivers and on our own—and he enjoyed it as much as we did. We were his captive, and delighted, audience in the early years. Then, in junior high, we acquired a car pool—several classmates of mine. Dad became the captive, and interested, audience on those morning commutes.

Dad was curious about everything and interested in everything. He loved to talk about what he was doing and about what he was going to do. But he was a good listener, too. Nothing was wasted on him. Things that he observed or experienced throughout his life would later find their way into every part of his product. He learned from his successes, and he learned from his failures. He learned from listening to all kinds of people—even us adolescent girls. And he learned from observing people—what they did, what they enjoyed doing.

From childhood on, he was an aspiring entertainer—the class artist, the class clown. His family—his parents, three older brothers, and one younger sister—were of a much more serious nature. But they were always wonderfully supportive of him, and I think that they all must have been rather delighted with him. His sister, my aunt Ruth, said to me, "We never knew what he was going to do next."

But Dad was very serious about everything he was doing, too. Nothing he did was, in his mind, idle play but had a purpose. His family must have recognized that in him and respected it. My uncle Roy, who was the closest in age to Dad of all his three brothers, was especially nurturing and encouraging, financially as well as emotionally, throughout Dad's youth. He did, in fact, cast his lot with this little brother and became his partner for life—and beyond, actually.

This strong family that Dad was a part of had a great deal to do with the kind of man Dad was and the kind of values he had. The family lived together and worked together. They shared hard times—and there were many—but they also enjoyed simple pleasures like pride in their orchards, the excitement of trains passing by, the spirit of community at threshing time, visits from beloved relatives. Love and respect for family and a high regard for honest work and for his fellow man characterized everything Dad did. He never played down to anyone or gave less than what he hoped was his best effort. He always strove to give better and to give good value.

Dad was not really a "celebrity" until his entry into television, when he became the host of his own show on ABC. He took his "lead-ins" very seriously, but he also had great fun with them. Once more he was, in a sense, standing up in front of the class, offering entertainment. The man you've seen on television is the real man—warm, earnest, with a bit of ham actor popping out at times.

Sharon and I found it difficult at first to share this celebrity father with the world. Other young people seemed to feel that he belonged to them, too, and I think that we were a bit jealous. We wanted to keep him to ourselves.

But then we both grew up and began to understand and appreciate his fame and the interest that so many others had in him and his work. I am willing now, and eager, to share him with those who seek to know him better. His was a good life, well lived. We loved him dearly and are proud of him and of his legacy.

Diane Disney Miller
January 1996

EARLY YEARS

"My dad worked as a carpenter in Chicago on the World's Fair Building. Out of his earnings he and my mother saved enough money to go into business. Mother drew the plans and my dad would build all the houses. He was doing that when I was born, which was on December 5, 1901."

The fourth son of Elias and Flora Call Disney was born in this house on Tripp Avenue in Chicago. Keeping his promise to name the next male child after their minister friend, Walter Parr, Elias named the boy Walter Elias Disney.

In many ways Walt Disney was a typical boy born at the beginning of the twentieth century. He had three brothers, Herbert, Raymond, and Roy, and one sister, Ruth. His parents were hardworking and instilled that quality in their youngest son.

Like other boys of that era, Walt worked at many jobs, including newsboy and later, "news butcher," selling papers and refreshments to passengers during train trips.

Walt spent much of his childhood on the family farm in Marceline, Missouri. The farm and its orchard represented a golden time for him.

"We had every kind of apple growing in that orchard. They were *that* big! People came from miles around to see our orchard–and to see these big things."

Walt with his sister, Ruth.

Walt, Flora, and Ruth Disney.

Although his mother taught him to read, Walt did not attend school until he was almost seven years old. Elias Disney felt it would be convenient to send Walt and Ruth together when she came of school age.

Walt's first-grade class. Walt is seated in the front row, center.

"Things got pretty tough on the farm. My dad had a sickness and he decided to sell it. He had to auction all the stock and things. It was in the cold of winter and I remember my brother Roy and myself going out and going all around to the different little towns and places tacking up posters of the auction. So my parents sold out, took the money, and went to Kansas City."

Walt in Kansas City.

"When I was in school in Kansas City, and later in Chicago, I was both stage- and movie-struck. [Walt Pfeiffer] and I worked up skits and competed in amateur theatrical contests. We also put on specialty acts I had staged and directed."

Two Walts: Walt (right) with his friend Walter Pfeiffer, who later worked at the Disney Studio for thirty-seven years.

"My dad bought a *Kansas City Star* route. A newspaper route was quite a thing. They gave me a small one. I must have had fifty customers. In the winter, we'd go out at three-thirty in the morning in a blizzard, or in pouring rain—it didn't matter. And I did that for six years. It was tough."

"In the meantime, my brother Roy had joined the navy. He used to come down and visit from Great Lakes and, gee, he looked swell in that sailor's uniform."

Filled with patriotic enthusiasm, many young men wanted to enlist during World War I. Walt tried to join his brother Roy in the navy, but the recruiter turned him down because, at sixteen, he was too young.

"Finally this kid came in to me, very excited, and he says, 'There's sumpin' just forming here that you and I can get in.' I said, 'What is it?' and he said, 'An ambulance unit.' So we went down and signed up.... And we were on our way to France."

Walt and his brother Roy.

Walt's passport photo. The Red Cross accepted him only because he had made himself a year older by changing the birth year on his passport application from 1901 to 1900.

"I had pictures all over my truck. I had a doughboy I used in a lot of these cartoons...this doughboy with this beaming face."

Walt's duties in France included transporting personnel and supplies. Once Walt's truck broke down and he stayed awake for two days and two nights guarding his valuable cargo of beans and sugar.

"I was in Paris the third of September when Pershing pulled out. The whole headquarters company left. And all the guys I knew had gone. Paris had been this exciting thing with all these soldiers, but suddenly there wasn't a soldier to be seen. And I suddenly became very lonesome. So I went in and put in a request to be discharged. Then I left shortly after that to come home."

"The things I did during those ten months I was overseas added up to a lifetime of experience.... I know being on my own at an early age has made me more self-reliant."

Walt returned to Chicago from France. His father had a job lined up for him, but Walt said,

66 'Dad, I want to be an artist.' And my dad, he just couldn't buy that. 99

So Walt left Chicago to join Roy in Kansas City, where he got a job in animation.

Walt (center) as a young animator at the Kansas City Film Ad Company.

66 So I went into this Kansas City Film Ad Company and that was where I got started in the animation business. With the first money I made, I bought myself a motion picture camera called the Universal. 99

66 I wanted to experiment...making theatrical cartoons, so I started experimenting at night. 99

66 I was desperately trying to get something that would take hold, catch on. I was thinking, If I had something with a novel twist to it, I might crack the market. 99

An actual scene from *Alice's Wonderland*, the first Alice Comedy, in which Walt introduces the young actress Virginia Davis to the cartoon world she is about to enter. The animation drawings were designed with large white areas. The actress portraying Alice was filmed against a white backdrop, making it easy to combine the cartoon and live-action scenes.

At the time Walt started in the animation business, people were making cartoons in which characters leaped from the drawing board into the real world.

"So I thought of a reversal. I took a real person and put him into the drawing, you see? I found a little girl that had been posing for some of the commercial things. But I couldn't get anywhere with it, and the company began to collapse. There was no money coming in, so we finally had to go into bankruptcy."

"I'd failed. But I learned a lot out of that. I think it's important to have a good, hard failure when you're young."

"I wanted to get to Hollywood."

1920s

"It was a big day when I got on that California Limited and came to Hollywood. It was in July 1923; I was twenty-one. My suitcase was kind of a frayed cardboard one. But I had a checkered coat, and my shirts were clean.

"Now, my brother Roy was already in Los Angeles and neither of us could get a job. We solved the problem by going into business for ourselves. We established the first animated cartoon studio in Hollywood. "

Roy and Walt in a California orange grove, 1923.

Walt and Lillian Bounds Disney honeymooning in Washington, 1925.

The 1920s saw many changes in Walt's life. He and his brother Roy became business partners in 1923. Both brothers married women who would become their lifetime partners. And they saw their little studio grow in staff and size, as they moved from a storefront on Kingswell Avenue to a larger space on Hyperion Avenue.

The era started with Walt's first business failure back in Kansas City. It ended with his first big success, when Mickey Mouse premiered in the first cartoon with synchronized sound.

"For two months I tramped from one studio to another. I was willing to start at the top; you know– as a producer, as a director, as a writer, even got down to where I was willing to take a job as a laborer–anything to crash those magic gates of big-time show business."

New employees as well as former coworkers from Kansas City joined the Disney brothers' growing animation Studio. From left are Ub Iwerks, Ham Hamilton, Walt, Thurston Harper, and Roy, about 1924.

Finally Walt sent his pilot film of *Alice's Wonderland* to a distributor who gave him a contract to produce the series. In October 1923 the Disney Brothers Studio began operation.

Traditional tin cans are replaced by even more resonant attention-getters at Roy and Edna Disney's wedding in 1925.

Posing with his young star Margie Gay and other featured performers at the second Studio location, on Hyperion Avenue, 1926.

Walt produced fifty-seven Alice Comedies between 1923 and 1927. He then began a series of twenty-six cartoons featuring Oswald the Lucky Rabbit.

Accompanied by their wives and sister, Ruth, Walt and Roy pose in front of their first Hollywood Studio on Kingswell Avenue, 1925.

Margie Gay, Walt's third Alice, is dwarfed by the stacks of artwork needed to produce animated cartoons.

"Several years of producing one series after another on a shoestring budget followed. Then sound on film panicked the industry... and Mickey Mouse came into our life...."

Walt, Ub, Rudy Ising, and Hugh Harman find time for some high jinks on the blank backdrop used for shooting live action that would then be combined with animation.

Walt's early business partner from Kansas City, Ub Iwerks, reunited with his friend in California and established himself as the Studio's top animator. The first Mickey cartoon put into production, *Plane Crazy*, was entirely animated by Ub.

"He popped out of my mind onto a drawing pad on a train ride from Manhattan to Hollywood, at a time when the business fortunes of my brother Roy and myself were at lowest ebb and disaster seemed right around the corner."

"His first actual screen appearance was at the old Colony Theater in New York on November 18, 1928, in *Steamboat Willie*. I did the voice."

Clockwise from upper left are Johnny Cannon, Wilfred Jackson, Les Clark, Jack Cutting, Carl Stalling, Walt, and Ub.

21

1930s

"Mickey was the first cartoon character to stress personality. I thought of him from the first as a distinct individual, not just a cartoon type or symbol going through a comedy routine. Mickey was simply a little personality assigned to the purposes of laughter."

The popularity Mickey Mouse achieved with the release of *Steamboat Willie* continued throughout the 1930s. Walt Disney's name was becoming associated with a quality of animated filmmaking that was far in advance of other studios. More and more artists started to join the growing Disney Studio, attracted by the opportunity to work in this exciting new medium.

Walt's dedication to improving the technical aspects of his films resulted in an equal emphasis on improving the artistic skills of his staff. He set up art classes for them and even gave them money for supper so they could have a meal before returning to the Studio to continue their studies.

Walt in his office.

Lillian and Walt at home with their chow Sunnee.

"By nature I am an experimenter. So with the success of Mickey I was determined to diversify. I had another idea that was plaguing my brain. It was *The Silly Symphonies* [a cartoon series based on musical themes]."

"I had a picture in the works called *Flowers and Trees*. I'd finished about half of it in black and white. But I just felt that color would do so much for the cartoon medium that it was worth doing the picture over. And fortunately for me it did hit. It went on and won an Academy Award—the first cartoon to win an Academy Award."

Walt and Roy display their first Oscar for the creation of Mickey Mouse and the Academy Award certificate for *Flowers and Trees*.

"Well, the *Three Little Pigs* followed sometime in early 1933, and we got a very warm reception from the audience."

Music played an important role in the Disney films. A piano and composer were frequently a part of story discussions.

As the popularity of the Disney cartoons spread around the world, the Hyperion Studio staff continued to grow.

Walt was told by a doctor to build himself up by starting an exercise program. He took up swimming, boxing, golf, horseback riding, and polo.

Both Walt and Roy were concerned with the quality of the merchandise that carried the Disney name. Here Walt examines playing pieces from the *Mickey Mouse Waddle Book* produced in 1934.

The royalties from Mickey Mouse merchandise not only helped bring needed revenue into the Disney Studio, but Mickey is credited with saving some well-known manufacturers from bankruptcy during the harsh Depression of the 1930s.

In 1934, happy parents at last, Walt and Lillian pose with their first daughter, Diane, who was born in late 1933.

66 I saw the handwriting on the wall early – the short subject was just a filler on any program. I felt I just had to diversify my business. Now, if I could crack the feature field, then I could do things. 99

❝ In 1935 I said, 'We're going to make a feature.' I had done a little story research on different fairy tales, and *Snow White* was one of them. I thought it was a perfect story. I had the heavy, I had the prince and the girl, the romance, and I had the sympathetic dwarfs. **❞**

Walt wanted each of the Dwarfs to be a distinct individual. The solution was to create names for them that would reflect their personalities.

❝ I wanted no doubt about the personalities. So when I had Bashful, he was bashful; when I had Happy, he was happy; I had Dopey – he was dopey. **❞**

Walt remembered that when he had first come to Hollywood, he had seen celebrities attending a premiere.

66 And I just had a funny feeling. Just hoped someday they'd be going into a premiere for a cartoon. 99

The premiere for *Snow White and the Seven Dwarfs* proved to be as great as any producer could have hoped for. And the enthusiastic response from the public made the film the highest-grossing movie until that time – quite a record, when it is noted that the average cost of a movie ticket in the 1930s was twenty-three cents, and many children's tickets cost a dime.

66 We had a big premiere at the Carthay Circle Theatre. A big, grand Hollywood premiere. All the Hollywood brass turned out for a cartoon. 99

Walt was a master storyteller. Early in 1934, he had gathered his staff together and told them the story of *Snow White and the Seven Dwarfs*, acting out all the parts so vividly that they were all eager to embark on the challenges of creating the world's first animated feature.

Walt was equally inspired when he had an audience of only one. He sat at his nephew Roy's bedside one evening and told the tale of *Pinocchio* so dramatically that the young boy could visualize every fantastic adventure of the puppet brought to life by the Blue Fairy's magic and his uncle's storytelling ability.

At the Studio, Walt demonstrates his storytelling skills during a story conference for *Pinocchio*.

"*Snow White* cost a million four hundred thousand. *Pinocchio* went up and cost two million six hundred thousand dollars before I got through with it. You see, we began to find out we could do things... and – boy! – we went into effects, and things were very costly."

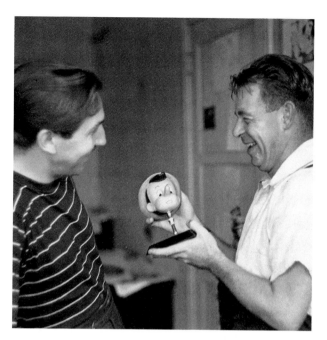

Walt involved himself in every aspect of *Pinocchio* production, from story development and the selection of songs to scene layouts and character animation. The inspiration he brought to his work continued to attract talented men and women to his Studio. Together, they lifted the cartoon to the level of art.

❝*Pinocchio* was released at a time the world was kind of collapsing. So it didn't do well.**❞**

World War II began in Europe in 1939, and people in the United States became preoccupied with the concerns of wartime. *Pinocchio* did not turn a profit when it was first released, in 1940. But many reissues later, both as a film and on video, *Pinocchio* has made back its cost many times over. More important, people consider it one of Walt's best films.

As he talked his artists through the story of *Pinocchio*, Walt played each of the characters. Here he acts out the scene in which the little puppet sinks to the bottom of the sea in search of his father, Geppetto.

1940s

"My brother called me and said that we owed the bank four and one half million dollars. And I began to laugh. And he said, 'What are you laughin' at?' And I said, 'I was just thinking back when we couldn't borrow a thousand dollars.'"

The public probably would have been very surprised to learn what a difficult time Walt faced throughout the 1940s. After all, they were still enjoying his feature-length cartoons and shorts regularly in the movie theaters. Disney books and merchandise were seen everywhere and were cherished items in children's toy collections.

Because of World War II and the Studio's support of the war effort, plans for some animated features were shelved. For the rest of the 1940s, Disney "features" were actually short cartoons packaged together or less expensive films combining animation with live action.

Still, with the profits from *Snow White*, Walt had been able to build a new Studio.

During a recording session Walt speaks for Mickey, while Clarence Nash's talents give voice to Donald Duck.

Walt helps celebrate his father's eighty-first birthday.

Final production on *Pinocchio* was completed at the new Studio in Burbank. The buildings were carefully designed to provide the best possible conditions for people working in the specialized field of animation.

Walt and Roy study architectural plans.

In February 1940, Pinocchio officially joined the Studio's stable of animated stars.

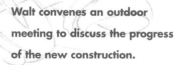
Walt convenes an outdoor meeting to discuss the progress of the new construction.

66 The Studio ended up costing us – with furnishings, buildings, and everything – around three million dollars. But I had all these pictures in the works – *Pinocchio*, *Bambi*, and *Fantasia*. **99**

Walt looks out over the Studio

During World War II the Studio's artists designed thousands of insignia for U.S. servicemen and -women and their allies.

❝ *Fantasia* to me is a whole new opportunity. For my medium it opens up unlimited possibilities. Music has always played a very important part since sound came into the cartoons. Now the full expression that comes from the new Fantasound [an early type of stereophonic sound] opens up a whole new world for us. ❞

Looking at backgrounds from the innovative concert feature *Fantasia*.

Walt at his piano in 1941. Visible are animator models of *Fantasia* characters and some characters the public wouldn't see until many years later, including Michael from *Peter Pan* (1953) and an early design for Lady from *Lady and the Tramp* (1955).

Walt and Lillian meet with reporters at the Burbank airport before departing for South America. The popularity of the Disney films throughout South America made Walt an effective representative for the U.S. Good-Neighbor Policy.

Reviewing a model sheet for the *Dumbo* clowns.

66 *Dumbo* sort of grew. It started with a little idea, and as we kept working with it, we kept adding, and before we knew it we had a feature. It was really a fun picture. 99

Walt contemplates the models of his flying star alongside the Dumbomber, which appears in the film's conclusion.

" A little thing happened in *Bambi*. My daughter, Diane, was quite a reader. She was about nine years old. She had read the book. When I finished the picture and brought it home and ran it, she cried when Bambi's mother was killed. And afterward she said to me, 'Daddy, why did you have to kill Bambi's mother?' And I said, 'Well it was in the book, dear.' She said, 'There were plenty of things in the book that you changed. Why couldn't you have changed that?' She had me there. **"**

Two fawns representing Bambi and Faline were kept on the Studio lot for the animators to study.

Bambi was originally planned to be the second animated feature, following *Snow White and the Seven Dwarfs*. But the degree of realism Walt envisioned for this film created challenges that slowed down production.

66 I wanted to go beyond the cartoon. Because the cartoon had narrowed itself down. I could make them either seven or eight minutes long—or eighty minutes long. I tried to package things, where I put five or six together to make an eighty-minute feature. Now I needed to diversify further and that meant live action. 99

Walt and his young star Bobby Driscoll take time to examine a snake they've discovered on the outdoor set for *Song of the South*, a film that combined a live-action story with animated sequences of the Uncle Remus stories by Joel Chandler Harris.

Walt feels right at home in Granny Kincaid's cabin, built for the movie *So Dear to My Heart*, the story of a young boy on a farm at the turn of the century.

66 *So Dear* was especially close to me. Why, that's the life my brother and I grew up with as kids out in Missouri. The great racehorse, Dan Patch, was hero to us. We had Dan Patch's grandson on my father's farm. 99

Away from the Studio, Walt was able to enjoy spending time with his family and pursuing his many other interests.

The Disney family in 1948.

In front of their home in the Los Feliz section of Los Angeles with their poodle Duchess Disney.

Testing the train engine christened the Lilly Belle, after Walt's wife.

"I decided that all my life I'd wanted a miniature train and I made up my mind to have one, even if I had to make it myself. I went to the head of our Studio machine shop and told him about my ambition. Ward Kimball had given me a blueprint of an old-time engine and I asked the shop foreman, 'Do you think we can build a scale model from this?' 'Sure,' he said. 'Why not?' 'But I've never worked on a metal lathe,' I told him. 'Can you give me an hour to an hour and a half a day?' he asked. 'If you can, I'll teach you.'"

Walt during an outing with the riding club Rancheros Visitadores. Their horseback rides took them through the foothills between Los Angeles and Santa Barbara.

43

1950s

Walt, Diane, and grandson
Chris on the Tomorrowland
Autopia.

Walt in a Disneyland
company vehicle.

"Now, to do a good cartoon feature takes a lot of money. And I said, 'By hook or crook we've got to get going. We've got to get back in the business we were in before the war.'"

Roy Disney once referred to 1950 as "our *Cinderella* year." This was not only because the film had been released at the beginning of that year, but because Walt's insistence on returning to the classic fairy-tale format for an animated feature had paid off with both box office success and warm public acceptance.

It was the perfect way to start the decade that would see so many changes and growth in the types of family entertainment Walt and the Studio would be involved in. He began regular production of live-action features and he entered into weekly television with "Disneyland" and the "Mickey Mouse Club." And just as he had gambled on his company's future by producing the first animated feature back in 1937, he began a project that cynics were calling Disney's Folly: the creation of Disneyland the Park .

Walt's desire to return to creating animated features based on classic fairy tales resulted in *Cinderella*, which was followed by *Alice in Wonderland* and *Peter Pan*.

❝ I can't think of the pictorial story without thinking of the complementary music that will fulfill it. **❞**

Color stylists for *Cinderella* John Hench, Mary Blair, and Claude Coats.

Walt with composer Oliver Wallace, who wrote songs and background scores for many of the Studio's live-action and animated films.

Walt stands in front of the multiplane camera, which was developed at the Studio to give an illusion of depth in animated films.

Reviewing art with members of the
story team, Winston Hibler, Ted Sears,
and Ed Penner.

Walt shows early concept paintings for
Alice in Wonderland to Kathryn Beaumont,
the young actress who would provide
Alice's voice.

With Marcia Sinclair in the Ink and Paint
Department, where animators' drawings
are transferred onto acetate and painted.

"The idea for a Disneyland came along when I was taking my kids around to these kiddie parks. We used to go out every Saturday and Sunday. I took them to zoos; I took them everywhere. And those were some of the happiest days of my life."

Checking out the pirate galleon that would fly visitors to Never Land on the Peter Pan attraction.

> 66 And while they were on the merry-go-round, I'd
> be sitting there trying to figure what you could do.
> I thought we ought to have a three-dimensional
> thing that people could come and visit. 99

The Seven Dwarfs'
cottage, Geppetto's
workshop, and the
Old Mill getting
readied for Storybook
Land.

Examining details on
the model for the
Mark Twain riverboat.

> 66 I had a little dream for Disneyland
> adjoining the Studio. I couldn't get
> anybody to go along with me
> because we were going through this
> financial depression. But I kept
> working on it and I worked on it
> with my own money. Not the
> Studio's money, my own money. 99

Reviewing the layout for Disneyland.

66 I think what I want Disneyland to be most of all is a happy place – a place where adults and children can experience together some of the wonders of life, of adventure, and feel better because of it. **99**

66 The way I see it, Disneyland will never be finished. It's something we can keep developing and adding to. I've always wanted to work on something alive, something that keeps growing. We've got that in Disneyland. **99**

66 We believed in our idea – a family park where parents and children could have fun together. **99**

Disneyland opened on July 17, 1955. Its popularity and success became the model for future Disney Theme Parks in Florida, Tokyo, and Paris.

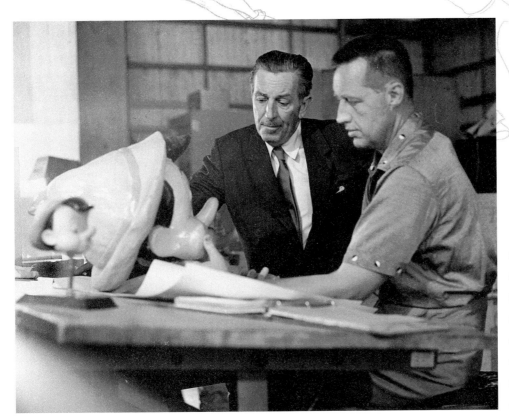

A three-dimensional head of Pinocchio is developed for Disneyland using a maquette model that had served as reference for animators working on the film more than a decade earlier.

Walt and Sharon enjoy ice cream at the Park.

And I knew that if I did anything like the Park, that I had to have some kind of medium like television to let people know about it.

In Walt's contract with the American Broadcasting Company, he produced both the weekly "Disneyland" series and the "Mickey Mouse Club," which began its original three-year run as an hour show Monday through Friday.

66I said, 'Well this television thing can be the greatest thing, because we will be going direct to the public.'99

66But we won't throw any piece of junk at the public and try to sell 'em. We fight for quality.99

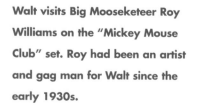

Walt visits Big Mooseketeer Roy Williams on the "Mickey Mouse Club" set. Roy had been an artist and gag man for Walt since the early 1930s.

Walt filmed the introductions to his weekly television series in an "office" built on a soundstage.

Donald Duck guest stars with Walt during a "Disneyland" episode.

66 It was television that helped us get *Lady and the Tramp* out to the public. And through getting it to the public and showing them little bits of it was what gave the picture a chance to be successful. And when they came to the theater and saw the picture, they were not let down. 99

Walt relates the history of animation to his television audience.

In 1956 the town of Marceline, Missouri, welcomed two hometown boys, Walt and Roy, on their return visit. It was a fun trip for the Disney brothers, who renewed their acquaintance with friends and neighbors and revisited scenes from their youth.

Roy had worked on the railroad and had gotten his teenage brother a job as news butcher during train trips. As an adult, trains still held a fascination for Walt.

Walt and Roy take a wagon ride over Marceline farmland, as they had done in their youth.

The letters WD are still visible on the school desk where Walt carved his initials as a young boy.

Walt and Edna find that things seem to have "shrunk" from their school days.

66 Well, it's wonderful to be back. I feel so sorry for people who live in cities all their lives and don't have a little hometown. I do. I'm glad my dad picked out a little town where he could have a farm, because those six years that we spent here [were] memorable years. 99

1960s

"There's enough land here [in Florida] to hold all the ideas and plans we could possibly imagine. It will never cease to be a living blueprint of the future, where people actually live a life they can't find anywhere else in the world."

Several weeks before his death, at age sixty-five, Walt stepped before the cameras for the last time. In this, his final filmed appearance, Walt shared his plans for his most ambitious project: Walt Disney World and EPCOT. Sadly, he was unable to personally see his dream brought to life. He died on December 15, 1966.

Walt's prediction that he had set something into motion that would continue after he was gone has proven prophetic. The company he and his brother began in 1923 continues to be associated with outstanding family entertainment. And Walt Disney lives in the hearts of people around the world to whom he has brought joy and laughter and the conviction that, when you truly believe, dreams do come true.

Walt enjoyed sharing his television hosting duties with members of the animal kingdom, and in spite of their unpredictability (or perhaps because of it), he always had fun with these segments.

"I have learned from the animal world a renewed sense of kinship with the earth and all its inhabitants."

Walt frequently lent both his personal support and the resources of the Studio to charitable causes.

Walt and Roy with early storyboards for *The Jungle Book*, the last animated feature Walt would supervise.

Walt on the island of Crete during the filming of *The Moon-Spinners*, a romantic mystery that took full advantage of its beautiful Mediterranean island setting.

Walt examines a model, along with some Imagineers, the name given to designers of the Disney theme parks.

66 Boy, when you think of the details we get into these days to make a picture. Why, we used to knock these things out every two weeks... well, no more than a month, anyway. 99

Walt shares some memories and laughs with Ub Iwerks and Les Clark, as they look at story sketches for *The Karnival Kid*, a 1929 Mickey short they had all worked on.

Chris and Joanna Miller join their grandfather in
a Disneyland holiday parade.

66 Well, after forty-some-odd years
in the business, my greatest reward,
I think, is I've been able to build
this wonderful organization. Also,
to have the public appreciate and
accept what I've done all these
years – that is a great reward. 99

January 1, 1966. As Grand Marshal of
the Rose Parade in Pasadena, Walt and
Mickey wish millions of television
viewers a happy New Year.

66 And the public has been my friend. 99

BIBLIOGRAPHY

To discover more about the lives of Walt and Roy Disney and the history of The Walt Disney Company, look for these books at your local library:

Fanning, Jim. *Walt Disney*. New York. Chelsea House Publishers, 1994.

Finch, Christopher. *The Art of Walt Disney*. New York. Harry N. Abrams, 1973 (revised, 1995).

Greene, Katherine and Richard. *The Man Behind the Magic*: *The Story of Walt Disney*. New York. Viking, 1991.

Maltin, Leonard. *The Disney Films.* New York. Hyperion, 1995.

Miller, Diane Disney, and Pete Martin. *The Story of Walt Disney*. New York. Holt, 1957.

Smith, Dave. *Disney A to Z: The Official Encyclopedia.* New York. Hyperion, 1996.

Thomas, Bob. *The Art of Animation: From Mickey Mouse to Beauty and the Beast*. New York. Hyperion, 1991.

Thomas, Bob: *Walt Disney: An American Original*. New York. Hyperion, 1994.

ACKNOWLEDGMENTS

This book was made possible by the generous support of many co-workers and friends. We would like to thank Ellen Friedman, Howard Reeves, and Lauren Wohl at Disney Press for making it all possible. Researching any book about the Disney family or the history of The Walt Disney Company is made easier and pleasurable by the organizational skills and helping hands at The Walt Disney Archives: Lizza Andres, Collette Espino, Becky Cline, Dave Smith, Ed Squair, and Robert Tieman. At The Walt Disney Feature Animation Research Library, Larry Ishino, Ann Hansen, and Vivian Procopio with their customary friendly and efficient service, helped us locate the animation drawings that enhance these pages. Jeanette Steiner and Brent Ford are colleagues whose talents are always willingly shared.

And we would like to thank Diane Disney Miller for her warm and encouraging support of this project.

Kenneth Shue
Janice Kawamoto
Russell Schroeder
February 1996